TELL ME

Again

The Cry of the Children

Dr. Patricia Morgan

Destiny Image₀ Publishers, Inc.
P.O. Box 310
Shippensburg, PA 17257-0310

ISBN 1-56043-180-6

For Worldwide Distribution
Printed in the U.S.A.

Destiny Image books are available through these fine distributors outside the United States:

Christian Growth, Inc.
Jalan Kilang-Timor, Singapore 0315

Successful Christian Living
Capetown, Rep. of South Africa

Omega Distributors
Ponsonby, Auckland, New Zealand

Vine Christian Centre
Mid Glamorgan, Wales, United Kingdom

Rhema Ministries Trading
Randburg, Rep. of South Africa

WA Buchanan Company
Geebung, Queensland, Australia

Salvation Book Centre
Petaling, Jaya, Malaysia

Word Alive
Niverville, Manitoba, Canada

This book and all other Destiny Image and Treasure House books are available at Christian bookstores everywhere.

Call for a bookstore nearest you
1-800-722-6774
Or reach us on the Internet:
http://www.reapernet.com

Part 1

Forgotten SORROW

The forgotten...dead?
Their blood cries out to us from the ash heaps
behind the abortionists' slaughterhouses.

Their cries come to us in the nighttime...

Forgotten?
How can we forget when their voices come to us
from the law courts?
From Washington?

1

How can we forget?
When our empty wombs ache for a child?
When our full breasts heave to give him milk?
When our aching hands long to soothe his brow?

How can we forget?
When their spirits return to the God who breathed
His life into their bodies?
When the words spoken by God for them still
echo across the airwaves and through the ages?
When the creative eyes of the Creator God still
roam to watch them grow?
And when the father hands of the Father God
still reach down to wipe away their tears?

Tell Me Again

*In 1992, 1,359,145 legal
abortions were performed.*

And what of the mothers?
How can we heal their brokenness?
The brokenness of an empty womb?
Hopes dashed?
Lifeblood spilt?
"O God," they cry, "where is my little one?
"For still I hear his cry...

"Still I feel the flicker of his life within me,
and still I bleed...
the blood that should succor him...
the blood that should give him life...
still that blood

    drips,

        drips,

            drips...

                wasted...wasted...wasted.

2

"And with it goes my heart, my hopes, my love...
And still I feel the cold, cruel instrument of death
as it intrudes into my once protective body and
reaches upward for my child.
Still I sense and still I hear
the silent surprise of my child,
the quiet helpless cry of my little one...
Still I feel the ruthless crushing of his bones...
my life...
And then the painful passage of my broken child
not through a portal to light, and hope, and life,
but into cold death,
my 'choice'—not his!
Gone...but not forgotten.

Tell Me Again

"And now I remember...
And now I long...   . . .A mother
And now I weep...
It's a mother's memory, a mother's longing,
a mother's tears...

"O God," I pray,
"Did You say that You too still feel the pain?
Did You say that You too still hear my baby's cries?
Did You say that You too still see the blood...the
wasted, spilt lifeblood?

cannot

"And what is this sound of hope I hear?
Did You say that out of death You will create life?
That Your spoken Word of promise for my seed
will not return void to You?
That You will give me still another chance?
To offer my body a living sacrifice to You?
To bare my breast to a hungry child in need of its
life-milk?
To let my heart overflow with Your love and life?
To let my hands gather their tears and cries and
brokenness?

forget

"And let You breathe again
yet once again, Your Spirit-life?
Thank You, Father God.
Be it unto me according to Your Word."

her

nursing child

Tell Me Again

3

46% of single mothers receive public assistance

lost hope falls...

death claims
the life...

...the heir
of God's promises

...and the enemy laughs

The children die, laden and burdened with the death of those who gave them life, only their death comes more heavily and more swiftly!
And the gnawing teeth of pain pierce their bodies more relentlessly.
And though the will to live flickers like a starved, weak, little broken flame,
yet the claws of death sink more deeply and drain away the very life more greedily.

a Heritage of DEATH

5

And death claims the life and steals the heritage of the God who gave that life.
And the battle continues—
and lost hope falls to the ground and lies buried within that cradle grave,
and that child who should have become
　　　—the flower of God's love
　　　—the heir of God's promises
　　　—the executor of God's purposes
takes all with him to the grave.
And the enemy laughs!

Tell Me Again

ALONE IN THE

LIMELIGHT

I see them in the stark lights of the television camera.
They clutch the dress hems of their mothers
or shiver helplessly among the dingy, dirty bedsheets
or crouch behind a neighbor's leg
or answer with fear and with silent pleas a kind
policeman's probing questions...
While one angry, cursing, bleeding, careless, reckless
parent damns that other angry, cursing, bleeding,
careless, reckless parent!

The real victims of law-breaking parents are the children,
whose lives are forever scarred, whose own con-
sciences are deeply seared, whose childhoods are
callously stolen.
Yes, they are the victims.
And as a nation watches its favorite TV show
to savor, with sadistic interest, those poor wretches'
naked violence,
the children listen for more gunshots
and more familiar night shadows
and they too learn to hide the damning evidence
and they too turn the TVs on to watch their
favorite, painful TV scenes.
Except that the children are themselves
the principal victims
—of a nation's sadistic viewing pleasure.

Tell Me Again

7

*Every five minutes a child is
arrested for a violent crime.*

Do you

CHILD
That's Me

Did you call me? Miss?

Did I hear you call my name? Did you say, "Come here, child?" That's me!

What makes you sing so brightly in the mornings?

What makes your step so light, your smile so warm?

Tell me—do you know the answers to my unasked questions?

Do you know what makes my mother cry?

Do you know what makes my father stay away so much?

Do you know why I feel so guilty when I meet my uncle?

Will you stop a while and talk with me?

Tell Me Again

In the U.S., 3,857,888 children (6.2%) live in "distressed neighborhoods."

CHILD
That's Me

Oh yes, you teach me how to count and how to read, how to add and how to spell...

But do you know how often I forget your question?

Do you know the tears that blind me as I try to read?

10

So many thoughts fill my mind and make it heavy with pain...

My mother's tears.

My father's fears.

Rachel
WEEPING for
her children

Tell Me Again

CHILD
That's Me

May I tell you of my shame—
my own greatest pain?

Just when I think I'm understanding, you go on to something new.

Just when the light begins to shine, those dark shadows steal into my mind...and then...

The lesson's over and it's time for you to go...

Will you stop a while and hold me...

Close enough to see my tears and the scars I hide and...

Did you call me, Miss? Did you call my name?

"Child"—That's me!

Tell Me Again

11

*Every four minutes a child is arrested
for an alcohol-related crime.*

a community has been robbed

of yet another child...

kidnapped and abused...

"Go outside and call sister, Johnny!"

*"Mommy, sister is not outside. I see her bicycle
at the side of the road!"*

"Honey, jump in your truck and see if you can find Sissie."

Someone said he saw a man jump out of a black
pick-up truck and drag the nine-year-old,
kicking and screaming, into it.
That was two days ago...still no Sissie...
And a mother's total life has changed.
And an entire family has been raped.
And a community has been robbed
of yet another child.

Kidnapped...

13

They say they found her little body in the creek,
stone-cold dead in the creek, behind the housing
complex, and that the kidnapper-rapist
still roams our streets...

And Sissie's blood falls to the ground
while the earth reels in revulsion
and the Creator rises from His throne
and swears to avenge Himself of His adversaries.
And a nation is judged, smitten with a curse,
and our creeks are polluted and stain the
very heart of this nation.
Until...until redemption dues are paid
and redemption lambs are slain
and the doorposts and the lintels are
smeared with redemption blood...

for all of God's slain inheritance!

Tell Me Again

*Stepdaughters are more likely to be sexually abused
by other men, especially friends of their parents.*

ABUSE:

Guilt and Shame, Guilt and Shame

What brings guilt, shame, doubt, and fear to the image of a child? What robs a child of the sweetness and potential of God's image?

Lack of basic trust in significant adults results in loss of trust in self. A child's trust in others depends on the extent to which those adults meet the child's basic needs. These include physiological needs for food, warmth, and clothing, but also psychological needs—for security and comfort. The overriding need is for love that is giving, forgiving, and consistent.

15

A street child in a large city flees from home because of physical abuse by his father, repeated public spankings from his mother, and a chronic lack of food, love, and peace in his chaotic household. On the

Tell Me Again

30 children or more each day will be wounded from gunshot wounds

street, this seven-year-old joins a gang of street waifs. Soon targeted by older pedophiles, he is introduced to homosexuality and drugs in exchange for food in his bloated, empty stomach. His life is one of violent rage, forced sexual perversive acts, repeated physical misfortune, and disease, dirt, and disadvantage.

When a child is "offended" or "despised," that child suffers a loss of trust in the significant adult who should be giving love, nurture, mercy, and care to that child. Jesus warned us not to "offend one of these little ones" and to "despise not one of these little ones" (Mt. 18:6,10). Offenses include willful acts of commission or careless acts of omission that deprive the child from having his basic needs met. Despising a child includes scornfully cursing him; tearing down his character, reputation, or self-esteem; withholding his deserved rights or gifts; and abusing his spirit, soul, or body.

Jesus, in fact, enjoined His disciples to receive or to positively regard a child, to accept and acknowledge his personhood and his giftings, and to seek to meet a child's basic needs. The child is presented as one who stands in need of being received

Tell Me Again

and in a dependent posture before generous, kind, and accepting adults who do not take unfair advantage of that dependence.

A gifted, upper middle class seven-year-old is targeted by all the perverted, offending males of his family. It was first his older cousin, then his uncle, then his grandfather, then his uncle's friend—all of whom repeatedly assured him that "that's the way it is." He runs away and joins a gang of children fleeing the police. Then one night, along with others, he is taken to the mountains where the "public nuisances" are exterminated—to please the robbed shopkeepers and those who call themselves keepers of the peace!

17

The sanctions to be meted out to the offender are clear and unequivocal:

"But whoso shall offend one of these little ones which believe in Me, it were better for him that a millstone were hanged about his neck, and that he were drowned in the depth of the sea. Woe unto the world because of offences! for it must needs be that offences come; but woe to that man by whom the offence cometh" (Mt. 18:6-7).

Tell Me Again

22% of U.S. children live in poverty

Jesus pronounces a curse upon the one who commits the offense and declares the inevitable curse that befalls the nations because of offenses committed against the children. Jesus assessed the generational sin of offending the children and simultaneously pronounced inevitable judgment to men and to nations for sins against children.

Another seven-year-old girl is lied to by her poverty-stricken parents, "sold" to an "auntie," chained, and taken to a remote house pf prostitution. Soon disease-ridden, HIV positive, and oozing with open sores, she is ousted from the brothel to sit on the dingy roadsides, selling her broken body to depraved vagrants.

Why was the heart of Jesus so touched?

Why is the heart of God so vehemently moved to judgment when a child is abused, shamed, or neglected?
1. The image of God invested in a child preserves His own image, His name, and His reputation.

Tell Me Again

2. The image of God in a child reflects the purity of God's own person; His untarnished, open, divine countenance; and His wholeness and integrity. When the child's image is dulled, tarnished, or shattered in any way, then the world does not have an earthly image through which to view the image of the invisible God.

3. Whenever God duplicates His image in yet another little child, He puts His own image "on the line" and invests yet once more His divine hope for His love to be shed abroad in the earth through that "image." God does not want to lose even one child.

19

"Even so it is not the will of your Father which is in heaven, that one of these little ones should perish" (Mt. 18:14).

4. When God's image in a child is marred, then the Kingdom of Heaven is depleted. "For of such is the kingdom of heaven," Jesus said. The spirit of purity and humility in a child is the key to that righteousness, peace, and love of the Kingdom of God. To dispossess a child of that trusting attitude is to disenfranchise a Kingdom citizen of his Kingdom rights.

ON EDGE."

Tell Me Again

Men appear prone to blame themselves for any sexual abuse they experienced as children.

God hear the cryin

of all His children

A Caribbean Child Contemplates Life

TELL ME AGAIN

tell me again
how the children sit in the marketplace
an play their pipes for the parents to laugh
an how the children mourn for the parents to cry
an how those parents neither laugh nor cry
tell me again what kind of foolishness is this?
tell me again

tell me again
how one ole woman lived in a shoe
how they sey she had so many children she didn't
know what to do...
how she made them some broth without any bread
an how she "whipped them all soundly and sent
them to bed"
tell me again how come I don't believe one word of it!
tell me again

21

tell me again
how one young mother cud put her two children
in a car an send the car flyin into a lake—an then
say some black man t'ief the boy-children dem?

tell me again
how all the time God see an hear
an how this nation jus forget
an how come I still hear those children
cryin, cryin out for help
an how God prefer if the one who offend even

Tell Me Again

*In Asia tourism is a major contributory factor in
the growth of the sexual exploitation of children.*

one child put a big stone around his neck and
jump in the lake...before God get Him hand on him!
tell me again

tell me again
how Jesus stopped in the middle of preachin to
the big people to hear the disciples "shooin" away
the children
an how He sey, "Let the children come,"
how they must not stop dem
an how come the church basement so full up of
children?
an the pretty, plush front pews so pack-up wid big
people
an how Jesus really down in the basement with
the children!
tell me again

tell me again
how that death angel kill-off all Egypt firstborn
an how God warn Pharaoh
an how every Hebrew man had to find money to
buy dem lamb
an how he had to kill it
an how he had to put the blood on the doorpost or
else...
I can't believe God would-a kill de Hebrew-man
dem firstborn too!
yu betta tell me dat one again

tell me again
if that's why jails are full and sons are dyin

Tell Me Again

an if some parents still don't see why they have to
spend dem hard-earned money to buy one lamb
for any good-for-nothin sons
an if is true di death angel still passin...
tell me again

tell me again
how that frettin Pharaoh ordered those midwives
to kill-off all those boy-children of dem Hebrew slaves
an how the Nile ran red with those boy-children's
blood
tell me again

tell me again
how one woman save one Hebrew boy
an that Moses cry out at jus the right time
an how come Moses' mother's breast had milk
an Pharaoh's daughter's breast had none
an how that Moses eat an sleep in Pharaoh's house
tell me again

tell me again, Daddy,
how God hear the cryin of all His children
but how He spin around and get busy, busy when
the children with no father cry out to Him!
tell me again
why God is not jokin with me or you
an how those people who don't hear, will feel
an how nuff people goin to have to answer to God—
not to mention how much more questions I have
for You!
tell me again

Tell Me Again

*Ten of every 1,000 babies die
before their first birthday.*

rich gift of

pure sweet joy

SURPRISED

by Joy by Joy by Joy by Joy

A little melancholy girl sat and looked longingly
through a basement window
or was it prison bars?...

Joy comes

Why is my father so long in coming? And...
What will he bring for me?...
Will he...hold me when he comes? Give me a ride
on his bicycle perhaps?...

And so she sucked her thumb, and watched, and
looked...and looked...and waited...
Nothing surprised her—neither his coming, nor
his gift... No joy... And little by little the heart of
that little girl closed to the world...and closed to
the laughter...and closed to the joy that childhood
should bring.
And the years rolled by...
"No time for play"... "What's there to laugh about?"...
And those tears...so near they were...just below
the eyelids, just below the heart...just below the
hot, flushed face...the deep wounds rising in
waves—no, in spasms—from the little chest...was
it laughter? or was it tears?...would laughter come?
or would tears come?...
That same old pain in the middle of the heart...
no—in the middle of the stomach...
no—in the middle of the belly...with its long

in the

morning

Tell Me Again

25

*Approximately 95% of teenage prostitutes
have been sexually abused.*

oily rivers flowing down my legs and weakening
my knees and those spasms reaching upward to
my chest, my heart, my throat...
Was it joy or was it laughter?
But both were stifled...I would grant none of them
release. I would endure none of them.
"No time for play!" and "What's there to laugh
about?"
and "Stop that crying!" and "You look so ugly
when you cry!" So again the painful muffling of
them both—twin sisters— "joy and laughter."

And so the years
passed and the stoicism
grew!
The models—old staid
nuns, a mother who
pursed her lips and never
cried...but never laughed....
And a stiff determination
took root within that heart...to
achieve an internal balance—to
swing to and fro—but always,
always, always to stop just short
of pure joy; and always, always,
always to stop just short of
pure sorrow.
Then the spirit had to be
ruled and the soul dominated and the body brought
into subjection!
No time for laughter and

26

Tell Me Again

no time for tears,
distancing everyone who sought either of me.

But as my heart cried and longed to weep with
that lost child,
and as my soul longed to grieve for the death of
the children but always postponed and always
said "tomorrow,"
so my spirit yearned to laugh with my God
so my soul heaved to dance in the presence of my
laughing Father God
and so deeply did my body, my soul, and my spirit
mourn...
They mourned their need for disinhibition.
They mourned for full and free release.
They mourned for a chance to breathe life's joys,
to fully enjoy that full, pure release into carefree,
childlike welcome roars of laughter.

But last night a wonderful thing happened!
Crawling through the shadows and reaching
upward to the source of light...
Recklessly, passionately, childishly, and playfully, I
rushed into the presence of my Father
with His open arms, and laughing face; with outstretched love and joyful welcome—with a smile
that said:
"Yes, you can laugh; you can, you can! Let Me show
you how...come let us take our fill of joy and love
and laughter. Come let us reach deeply within
ourselves, back to your childhood,
and I will empty your heart of the very dregs
of pain.

Tell Me Again

27

*I Myself will rid you of the cloaks put on you by that
old Mother Superior, or by that serious, tension-
filled husband, or by that drunken father, or by that
determined, survivor mother,
and you will break forth into the sunshine of My
rich, pure joy.*

*"Let your body be subjected to that spirit of joy
and break forth—
let its fresh oil encase and, yes, entrap your heart,
and let its healing balm bring life to your spirit.
It's okay to be silly!
It's all right to laugh!...
loud and long, richly and fully...
And remember, My daughter, My own, dear daughter,
I too laugh—I laugh to see My little girl who still
waits,
and yes, I do bring you, My child, a gift—the rich,
rich gift of pure, sweet joy—Mine and yours!"*

28

Part 2

tell me

again

the women stand...

A Mother's
DETERMINATION

Always the women suffer.
Always they yearn...Eve waiting, waiting,
waiting for the appointed seed destined to crush
the head of the enemy.
And a woman waits and a woman yearns...

he

She longs for a son—that daughter of a
Shunammite. Her breasts ache to give comfort
and milk to a son of a priest—
that woman, without a name.

31

shall

And Rahab's body groans under the pain
of the men whose trifles provide for her
sons.

bruise

And Deborah's judgments impel and
constrain her for the place of battle—
for Israel's sons.

your heel

And Hannah yearns to cast off
shame and make a baby and an
ephod, and looks at Eli's rebel sons
and prays, "Not Samuel, Lord! Keep

BUT

you shall crush his

head

Tell Me Again

*Children of the street have only
little contact with families.*

him as the apple of Thine eye, for Israel waits and
buckles under the curse of wanton priests, infidel
prophets, and disobedient kings."

And I too yearn...
and the children die and Rachel mourns
and Leah's children die and Rachel mourns
and the land is ravished and Rachel mourns
and the men are silenced and Rachel mourns
and the women are dashed to the ground and
Rachel mourns.
And Bathsheba mourns the death of David's
son—
the one she did not seek but gladly bore—
the one she bore in shame but dearly loved.
And Hamutal mourns the captivity of her royal
seed as one prince after another is captured by
that Babylonian seed-devourer—
and still reels in pain at the straining rebellion
in her son!

And Zipporah circumcises from her very
soul the foreskin of her sons
and implores her Moses husband to pay
redemption blood
and thus protect those sons she loves.

And the land belches up again the
blood of our slain children...and
Rachel would not be comforted

Tell Me Again

because her children were not!
And the land groans and travails in pain for
Rachel's sons to manifest themselves, to call
forth their life and manifest the longed-for
dominion!

But God is looking for women
—strong enough to bear the weight of nationhood
—with tears enough to weep for a nation's men
—with breasts full enough to give milk to a
nation's children
—with arms strong enough to restrain our Eli
sons
—and voices bold enough to confront a
nation's brazen, law-breaking leaders
—for women generous enough to claim a
nation's bastard sons
—and wise enough to reclaim that coveted
vineyard...
for Naboth's landless, disinherited children.

Now, unafraid of that evil one who seeks
only to destroy her men, her children, and
her property, a woman remembers:
"*The kingdom of heaven suffereth violence,
and the violent take it by force*" (Mt. 11:12b).

She remembers Rahab...
She hid those spying Israelites and lied
to those bent on violent murder.

Tell Me Again

33

And Jael...
She offered Sisera milk when he asked for water.
But she hammered that nail good and hard and
killed that army captain!
And Deborah...
"Up," said she to Barak, the army general. "This is
the day to violently take the enemy!"

Yes, there is a time for weeping,
but *now* is the time for active, violent intervention.
Let's break that alabaster box!
Let's break those prison bars!
Let's saddle that ass and go get that Elisha
prophet to bring God's blessing to that dead
son!
Let's raid those Babylonian jails and set young
princes free!
Let Israel's mother mourn aloud,
let all our mothers mourn aloud;
but let us give our cry a voice,
for in Ramah it says a voice was heard!

Until...
Till the hoarse voices of the children crying
will no more be heard.
Till the stinking breaths and sweaty hands
of the rapist no more steal our children's
sweet virginity.

Till the hungry bellies of our children, no longer
bloated but firm and strong, are fed with the good
of this our land.
Till the children no longer have to cry in the marketplace in a vain attempt to pipe so that their
fathers can laugh, or to mourn so that their mothers can mourn.
Till selfish, "craven," murderous parents no longer
sell their children's bodies or mar their children's
image-stamp of God their Creator
or sear their own children's conscience.
Till Potiphar's wife leaves our young statesmen-
sons alone.
Until at the gate of every city,
and at the head of every street,
the women stand,
violent and tall and strong,
fearless and brave and bold,
articulate and proud and free.

35

LOVE never FAILS

love never fails

Tell Me Again

*Homicide is the third leading
cause of death for 5- to 14-year-olds.*

Today, I give you this child...

...My very own Godly seed!

God's Call to WOMEN

Not yours, you say?

You say you have no child and so turn away from this task to which I draw you? Today I give you this child! And that one! And yes, I give you the children of *this nation*!

I make them yours. For they are Mine! And My Father's heart earnestly longs to give them life.

I hear their cries in the nighttime while you sleep;

I hear their groanings in the daytime.

I see their ruthless cravings for that which does not satisfy them.

I see their brutal slayings. I listen to their muffled cries.

I see their spilt blood. It rises to Me from the ground,

and cries, and ever cries out for My mercy.

I hear their groanings. I hear, at times, their silly, inherited false pride!

Tell Me Again

Every six hours a teenager commits suicide.

37

And how I long to draw them to Myself—to life, and light.

How I long to make them indeed *My very own Godly seed*! How I hate the careless slaughter of My sons and daughters!

How I wait for deliverance of My seed!

Who will pluck them from the burning, burning?

Who will love them and enfold them with My arms outstretched?

Who will love them for *Me?*...

So that I no longer bear the reproach of those who laugh and say, "And where is their God?" and "Where is their *Father*?"

Will you go? Will you do it—for Me?

Listen! You can grab them out of the hands of the evil one, that seed-devourer! You can pull them out of the jaws of death. I gave you all authority. And today I give you even more—as you yield yourself to Me. I Myself will give you the strategy. I Myself will show you how...

Come, come, come, come,

and shed those burdens with which you cannot fight.

Tell Me Again

38

Come and shed those burdens that shackle and make you useless for the fight.

Come and leave at the cross those sins that separate us.

Come and leave at the cross those griefs that still encumber you,

for your griefs that you wrap around you only bring death and not life.

Come and leave at the cross the death that still eats at your own body and your own soul.

Come and leave at the cross your own pain. Come, come, come!

I will take away, yes, altogether away, that lingering loathsome memory that so blinds you to your present that you cannot wage a good warfare for My children—and yours.

39

Let us together rid ourselves of the pain of an empty womb;

come and wash yourself clean.

Then I Myself will reclothe you with a mantle of love and a strategy of care!

And then I will turn your eyes
to the sights I see—always.

And then I will turn your ear
to the sounds I hear—always.

Tell Me Again

A child dies from gunshot wounds every two hours.

And then I will cause you to feel the pain that My Father heart feels—always.

My seed—dying, slaughtered, buffeted, neglected

My seed—confused, betrayed, forgotten, still-birthed

My seed—aborted, slain, raped, sacrificed

My seed—gone—but *not forgotten*.

You ask for a burden?
Today I give you one!

It is My burden. Can you bear it? Can you too bear their dishonor? Can you too feel their confusion and their pain? Will you leave your comfortable dwellings of ease and walk with Me...to where they lie slain? Or do you too fear their enemy?

Come, come! I will clothe you with My love.

Let Me tell you of My love for them.

And you will walk with no fear in the fearsome shadows of your nation's streets and bring your children home.

Tell Me Again

You wish to hear of My love for them?

Were you there when I molded the dust to form their bodies?

Were you there when I breathed My life into them?

Were you there when I spoke a word for each of them?

Do you see that Word winging its way over time—

restless to find a place where it can be clothed with life and action?

For My Word does not and cannot return void to Me.

For each of them I have a task; for each a special place.

For each of them a song to sing; for each a special grace.

For each a task for them to do; for each an anointing too.

For each a crown, a kingdom rule; for each an honor due.

My children...

proclaimed

Tell Me Again

41

look,
your
breasts
are
full...

A CRY TO THE

BARREN AND CHILDLESS

The hungry voices of the children of my race call to me, their hands grasping for my breasts; their hungry, dry, parched lips reach up to me for life-milk.

Tell me your pain, my women. Do you not have enough?

Is your grief too great as you wrap yourselves in your own pain?

Do you lack the covering of men? Look, your breasts are full!

You say that you have no man and cannot bear a child?

Look at your breasts! How full they are of milk!

You say, "Why should I who have borne no child give milk to someone else's child?" Do you not turn when you hear a baby cry?

Do your breasts not tingle when you see a hungry baby grasp at the haggard, tired, empty breasts of a haggard, tired, empty woman?

Do your hands not ache to soothe their ruffled brows and reach to wipe away their tears?

OH YES, YOU DO...HAVE ENOUGH MILK FOR THE RACE BESIDES!

Tell Me Again

43

Of 13 million deaths of children under five, 8 million die from malnutrition.

bold defiance...

Let my sons go!

...defiant love

He's so good to me.

Defiant LOVE

From a Bold Mother's Heart

Faces like brass, willfully pitting defiant strength

[Faces like brass, willfully pitting defiant strength]

against the spoken words of rebuke and instruction, carnal flesh rises like sensuous fire to devour the Spirit's plaintive call to obedience and to the way of wisdom!

45

Faces bland and affect blunted,

[Faces bland and affect blunted,]

but underneath they boldly resolve to walk defiantly. Witha perceptibly calm but false facial expression, a challenging disobedience dares the instructor to demand response—for behind that flat affect is a torrent of loud, piercing, stilted willful words that say, "No more of your warnings! Freedom I

Tell Me Again

Homicide is the number one cause of death among black male teens.

God answers prayer.

demand, to do what I
will!"

come

Half-smiling, scoffing,

[Half-smiling, scoffing,]
scowling faces; unto
their muscles taut, unrelaxed,
cover a smoldering spirit of
me
recklessness and the stronger,
yet still weak and feeble, spirit of
low self-esteem and misguided
grasp for recognition from one's
smug and taunting peers.
you

46 And a father with patience repeats his warnings,
and paints yet once again, the deep dark entrap-
ments of the enemy who waits to ensnare the
Godly seed, God's prized possessions... who
—His legal heirs to Kingdom rulership
—His prime investment for their nation's wise
counsel are
—God's manifested sons for whom their land
groans.

weary and

And a mother watches open, gaping carnal flesh

[And a mother watches open, gaping carnal flesh]
and restless fluttering hearts
heavy laden,

Tell Me Again

and careless, brazen, lost innocence
and mocking, ensnaring frivolity
and foolish, scoffing provocation.

But stronger yet and immensely more eternal and
[But stronger yet and immensely more eternal and]
enduring is the certain call of God upon her children's lives!
Much, much more bold and resolute is the determination of their Father God.

Loud and much more impelling is the call of
[Loud and much more impelling is the call of]
destiny that deepens its roots in the purpose of
God and strengthens its own resolve to expedite
the lawful demands of God.
And that call of destiny receives fresh
new power to race toward the
called-out sons of purpose.
So together, destiny and

47

Tell Me Again

*Homicide is the second leading cause
of death for 10- to 24-years-olds.*

purpose link themselves to a mother's flintlike
affirmation
—that her sons will withstand those mild, weak
calls of her archenemy
—that her spoken, oft-repeated declarations of
God's revealed intentions for her sons will extin-
guish those fiery tongues of flaming flesh
and release those trapped wings of youthful
independence
and blast to shreds those of wanton foolishness.

tell me

And the strong call of my Father God will overwhelm

[And the strong call of my Father God will overwhelm]

48

the pitiful beckoning of lustful, prideful flesh.
And the battle for my sons will be won
—just because a woman's womb strained with
that growing life and
a woman's life-breath heaved to bring forth those
sons alive and
a woman's breasts tingled and swelled and gener-
ously nurtured those sons.
And still a woman's whole life demands more life
and kills that death
and lays hold on the horns of that altar

again

Tell Me Again

and dares any man, or any woman, or any false,
alluring god to come between the righteous,
Godly seed and the purposes of God!
And that same stormy spirit of violence with
which the violent take the Kingdom prevails
against the gates of hell
and laughs loud and long in the face of that weakened foe
—now destroyed, senseless, and stripped of tattered lewdness,
of gaudy, cheap enticements,
false facades, and empty promises! Ha! Ha!

That loud, long laughter first flickers deep down,
[That loud, long laughter first flickers deep down,]

49

down within that same womb that carried those
sons
and roars into a swelling crescendo of glory and
joy:

"Let my sons go!"
["Let my sons go!"]

And defiance lies wasted and obedient sons walk
free!

Tell Me Again

I shall give

depression

no more of my sons

The Battle
RAGES
for the Minds of Our Sons

Today I sat in church and watched with sadness as several ushers quickly removed a teenager, crazed, unmanageable, and mentally ill.

A declaration to the spirit of mental illness...

51

The toxic blend of those occultic, heathen spirits
and our ancestors' sacrificing of our sons to idol gods
fill their crowded, confused minds with the poison
of their depression, pain, rejection, and loss—
the sins of the fathers upon the sons?—
sends our male offspring raving mad and crazed
their lives weakened, their minds addled like a
broken egg...
and their bodies racked by electric shocks and by
drugs
and they seem to know not when death
comes!

Tell Me Again

Approximately 20% of all men have been sexually abused by the time they reach 18 years of age.

Ah! But longer lasting and much more
enduring is the strength of the sound mind of all
my godly forefathers.
More persistent is the fortitude of their well-being.
More secure is their rest in the true God of their
forefathers!

And so to the spirits of mental illness, I declare:
I shall give no more of my sons
to the mournful shadows of your fear and weakness!
I shall wrest them from your fangs and your fake
offerings of "ease" and "peace"!
I shall cast off and destroy every trace of your
ensnaring webs!
For planted deep in the rivers of living water of
my past are
the richer, stronger minds of my predecessors,
and the stronger fires of truth and life!

52

Tell Me Again

I will not listen to the lies that say,
"Don't bear seed.
Chances are they'll
inherit the crazy
weakness of
your past!"
But the
seeds
and the
power
of sound
minds
will rise within
their nation
—fully equipped to bear the
brunt of manhood
—fully free to love their women and birth their
children
—and fully empowered to father their nations as
well!

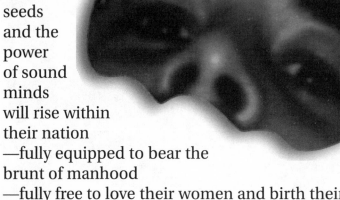

53

and
you
are
my
SON

Tell Me Again

*Adults who viewed domestic violence in the home
as children have a greater difficulty holding jobs.*

let us cry aloud...

"God save our children!"

DOMINION *Lost*
[to suicide]

I went into a nation and in the same edition of the daily newspaper, read two articles. One recounted the suicide of a well-known gentleman held in high esteem in the nation. The other told of the suicide, by hanging, of a 16-year-old boy.

Searching, searching, always searching to find the way, to find an answer...

55

Moving, moving...constrained to move forward into a long, long future—which takes up so much time.

Footsteps shortened, edging forward but wanting to stay in the present with all its own insecurities, always pretending to move forth into the future by doing the expected deeds, the daily common tasks without one single trace of hope inherited!
And the big, wide, ugly world beckons and opens its gaping, hungry mouth to devour the life of my sons.

Tell Me Again

Nearly 3,000 children and youth under 20 commit suicide each year using firearms.

And move forward they must—impelled not by a
divine desire to manifest God's compelling glory,
but only because they must keep on living.
No hope, no future awaits their intervention;
no tasks in view that will remain unaccomplished
without their intervention;
no evident need for that life-giving dominion that
young sons must impose upon their world.

The children move forward and into manhood
without a compelling call to claim their future,
without hope for a dominion lost, and without
one single dream of dominion
regained.

While the older of the species
disfigure their faces with their own
fear of that future,
and cry only with dismay at their
present, and thrive only on
mourning their own con-
torted past and their own
demanding present,
the children find them-
selves the victims of their
fathers' lost hope.
And childish innocence
becomes distorted
and hope becomes aborted
and still their children must
edge their way toward a
future that holds no rainbow
of glory,

56

Tell Me Again

a future that beckons only toward the dying old who wallow in their weakness—the weakness of lost dominion.

The nation is old and shattered by poverty and death and dying.
The nation is broken by its own curses—self-imposed—awaiting its own death, careless of its weak, young, hopeless sons whose dominion is blunted, whose compelling drive is confronted with millions, millions of lost and fallen dreams of all their forefathers.
They stumble over their fathers' lost hope.
They "buck their feet" on their fathers' discarded visions.
And still they must move forward toward an uncertain, gaping, hungry future that waits to engulf and devour the lives of my sons.

That future feeds itself on the hopes and dreams and visions of sons of promise!

And so the young man becomes captive to the beckoning call of that seed-devourer death who says, "Come, it's an easy road. It's easy, really! Here you will not even have to strive. I will show you the way. You'll find your feet just sliding easily, slipping painlessly toward that quiet, dark place where struggle no longer has a hold on you. This way is easy, quick— 'No problem'! Here you have no need for shame, yours or your fathers'; no longer will the jeers of foolish others mar your soul,

Tell Me Again

57

560 children of ages 10-14 are killed each year by firearms

you have no more of those long, long
days of searching, searching for lost hope
and elusive answers."

So a son believes the lie of that beguiling
death and yields himself to its enticing
snares and finds respite in its false calls
of "Peace, peace"—and a child turns
aside from a hopeless future into a
cold, dark death
that quickly devours the life of that son
and then laughs loud and long in the face of my
God whose heritage is the children...

And Jesus, Jesus, what are You going to
do about it, eh?

58

How do I calm my weeping soul?
How do I stop the angry tears?
How do I impose my life upon this death, which
lures the weak and hopeless sons of a weak and
hopeless nation?!
How do I expose this carnal, life-devouring mon-
ster death that lingers and waits to entrap my sons
and dares to slither around and hide behind fake
facades of false ease and momentary peace?

I must join with my women and "enlarge my
mouth over my enemies."
I must expose the hopelessness of the children.
I must expose the absence of their fathers' hope,
the stony silence of their mothers,

Tell Me Again

the careless hardheartedness of their leaders.
I must expose the utter, utter selfishness of their
forefathers, bent only upon their own survival, with
—no time for the little ones
—no time to tell them of that cruel beguiling
seed-devourer who wants only to engulf them in
his deadly grip
—no time to show them how to face the future
—no time to give them practice in skills to over-
come the one who steals their dominion.

These fathers have no altars built to testify of
God's good mercy and His sure covenant
and His unbroken promises to fathers' sons and
their sons too...
There are no dominion-bearers gifting their sons
born to dominate.
Oh! I must cry aloud and long and boldly
on behalf of the dying sons of this dying nation.
I must expose and pull aside the shadows that
seek to shroud our children's future.
I must shed light upon the hidden fields now
open and ready for the young to practice their
dominion.
I must tear back those dark clouds of death that
block the truth about those fields ready to be
worked into dominion—ready to be dominated
by my sons.

O Jesus, Jesus, move the spirit of silence off the men.
Tear away the chains of failure, which
entrap their fathers.

Tell Me Again

59

For if the fathers have no hope, then their very
sons will die entrapped
in the very chains that bind their captive fathers.

Women, women, come let us sing new songs of hope.
Let us arm ourselves with hope for this our nation.
Let us tear away those captive chains that bind
our hopeless men
and let us blast to smithereens those tattered shreds
of old, old, lost dominion!
Let us set our men free to ease the burden of their
own present
so they will brighten their sons' tomorrows.
Let us appoint a new song in Zion.
Let us walk those streets and dispel the darkness.
Let us cry aloud, "God, save our children!"
Let us raid those Babylonian jails and set our captive sons free.
Let us storm those mental institutions and set the
spirits of depressed sons free to dominate their
world.
Let us rid them of those false coverings of ease
—their minds shattered like broken eggs
—senses dulled to this old wretched world we
offer to them.
O Jesus, Jesus, help us bear the pain of all this loss...
And show us how You kicked down those gates
and led captivity captive!
Show us how You stormed those gates of hell and
teach us how You walked with hope masterfully,
steadfastly, without fear, toward Your own determined future.

60

Tell Me Again

You feared not death, You scorned the tempta-
tions of that evil one,
You conquered those weak Lazarus' graveclothes
and set the captives free of the chains of death.
And now we too must offer to You our own live
sons fit to rule,
born to crush the head of satan
born to set the captives free
born to bring a song to this groaning, groaning land.

Our sons...will impose their life upon the death
of this land;
they will manifest its longed-for release
and together You and I, Jesus, will watch this
nation rise
full of manifested sons of glory—conquering
death's shadows and overpowering its weak
enticements.
Life! Life! Life! And our sons' exulting laughter will
echo across their redeemed inheritance
and they will walk with proud head held high with
island pride
and their determined footfalls will make this old
land tremble with hope and pulsate with life.

Hope restored. Dominion regained.
"Flesh and blood" living sons singing happy songs
of victory...yours and mine!...
with hope enough for all their fathers' fathers,
with dreams enough for all their mothers' mothers,
with life enough for all of God's creation!

61

Tell Me Again

*Suicide is the third leading cause of
death among young people aged 15-24.*

but He is strong.

Searching for Identity
for the Children's Sake

"As He spake to our fathers,
to Abraham, and to his seed for ever."
From generation to generation—
God the Father ordained this plan
to bless His seed,
as He confirmed by oath the promises
He made to our godly fathers.

From generation to generation
the eternal God stretched man into eternity
through generations of seed;
blessings, anointings, callings, and gifts
transferring
from generation to generation...

And I look into the mirror and I see
an image there
not of one single race, but of many—
a collage of peoples, destinies, and histories...
Texture of hair, shape of nose, height of cheekbone...
a superficial blend of all their shapes and hues are
mixed up in a "callaloo" of genes passed down
from generation to generation.

63

Tell Me Again

Approximately 600,000 children grow up in
families existing at 50% of the poverty level.

But deeper, deeper yet within my spirit,
alive and burning still,
lie all the hopes and pride and struggle
of all my fathers.
Their prejudices, weaknesses, pain, and fear—
and their strengths, well-being, and hopes—
all vie for prominence.
And each lingering trait seeks pride of place
as if a war is taking place within my being.

And still my nagging, arrogant grandmother
wants her dregs of pride to rule
the quiet strength of my gentle, grave
grandfather.
And within my breast the two still battle for
dominion,
and I must quell the prideful spirit of the one
and allow at last the gentle strength of my
forefather to rule.

And I must walk with the tall Carib pride
of a great-grandfather whose existence all her
years my proud grandmother denied in shame,
for he was too poor, his mouth too broad, his skin
too dark, and his name—Subero—too "countrified."

But still that Carib yearning for survival
drags and draws me not to succumb
to foreign exploitation and disease, but to ensure
by will and wit the endurance of my seed
and my seed's seed.

Tell Me Again

64

And always, always I must quell the heaving,
unsolicited burst of pride that still
shoots itself like an arrow down through
the generations,
and I must cause to rise with a pure
gentle wave of warmth and passion
the humble dignity of my Oriental
grandfather.

And though I hate the smell of rum because it
rushes in with all its thousand memories of
bloodshot, bulging eyes and sneering,
cursing, angry lips,
yet that smell is linked to the one I loved
so well, and it was fully entwined within
my childlike spirit with the strength of manhood
and with the security of fatherhood.

65

And now my spirit must choose to forsake
the one—
the hated alcohol that brought
me pain—
and lay hold of the other only—
the strength and security of manhood and of
fatherhood.
For I must myself drink deeply of my
husband's intoxicating love and reach
for his fatherhood
for the sake of my seed!

Tell Me Again

Each year 500,000 teenage girls give birth.

Yes, Jesus loves me.

And though I hate and have revulsion for
the reckless, wanton curses of a sometimes
drunken father...
Still I find that...though I despise the
hated island rum,
its lurking spirit waits in the shadows
of my angry moments
to entrap me too in its outward gestures.
Its blazing anger, its reckless, painful,
and damning words
seem to come from the distant past
of all my memories of my two loud-mouthed,
obscene prostitute neighbors who
spat out scathing insults across
the fence—while I watched, and listened,
and learned...

66

And I fear that still that mocking
alcohol spirit moves
from generation to generation—
burning the throats and weakening
the male seed of the race.
So I must turn back that curse and
cut that umbilical cord of heady alcohol.
But I also must myself resist and
guard myself from its lingering behaviors,
lest I too dominate my seed with that
with which I was dominated...

Tell Me Again

So deep within my spirit do I bear the
life of my forefathers...
I long to walk barefooted on my African soil.
My breasts tingle with life-giving milk
when I see the hunger of my African babies
and my heart swells with pride for its
strong, independent black leaders,
mourns its shame at its poverty and division,
and soars in unresolved anger at its exploiters
and its selfish, careless leaders.

With what must I align my spirit—
one out of so many?
Do I revive my ancient Carib past?
Does it bring strength? For somewhere
within my heart I shun the weakness of your
death...
Do I wear the gold for which my grandmother
traded and sold her love...and which she
hid from her seed?

For now I look for my roots and cannot find them.
For long ago my grandfathers both ran away...
Was it to hide from responsibility for their little
black children?
To hide the gold they earned?
To retrieve their own lost past?

Tell Me Again

Every two hours a child is murdered.

And now, my daughters! And now, my sons!
You too must rise up strong and unashamed.
Shake off the prejudices, shame, and poverty
of your past—
but not its pride and rich dignity.
Keep that haughty aloofness from the crass and ugly;
nurse that strong desire to father many children!
For therein lies your hope of the heavenly Father's
promise
and your own hope for rich posterity!
Keep that determined love for ownership of land—
that strong sense of ownership of property—
that keeps you bound to your native land
and gives you the natural skill to govern
that land
which once held you as slave or as indentured
laborer...

Do not lose the fleetfootedness of your ancestors
their love of power over their bodies
their mastery and dominion over the petty elements
which they were born to rule.
For once men enslaved you, stole your land,
bought your bodies, and
their loins strained for those of your women!

Tell Me Again

Rise up to own the land where the seed of
your forefathers were sown
—in the secret back room of the little Chinese shop
—on the cocoa plantation...
Once you worked in the hot, hot sun of its
sugar estates.
Now make that land work for you and
bring its sweetness to your own table!

Rise up and give honor to the God of the Highest
—and to vindicate that ancestral asanti worship
of your great uncle
   "Bredda Willy—de preacher in de land
   with de candle in he hand
   and de ramgoat baptism!"
Break the old chains of shango, occultic
worship, and the shackles of blind Catholicism
of the ones who chose the monastic life and
cut off the possibility of seed!

Rise up and set your people free
from the occultism of your ancestors.
For still it snakes its venomous way down
the generations and
still it dares to claim the seed
and still it claps its hands at the
bloody mouths of the baby-mothers' wombs
and says, "Bear no more seed!"

69

Tell Me Again

*Sexual trauma has been found to occur frequently
in families where alcohol and violence occur.*

Take back the land that domination and fear
willed to the "mother church"
so that its power would be greater still
—to entrap more of your best seed.

Bring back to life again a rich pure
love to sail the ocean seas
—not in the damp, dark, stinking hulls
of the slave-masters' ships
—or as hungry-bellied indentured laborers
from the East,
but as a prophet son to conquer lands
and to make them the Master's footstool,
covered in His glory as the waters cover the sea!

For ah! you have washed your faces clean
and the stench of the dark belly of that ship no
longer clings to your bodies
and the odor of the occult no longer rises to the
Father God,
nor does the shame of your dastardly, forsaking
forefathers
or the silence and powerlessness of your grandmothers of old!

Now speak up for your people and
stand up for the right to life of all your nation's
children.
I see your future in their past
and you shall never again be ashamed.
For you bear within your body and your
spirit all their joys and strengths.

Tell Me Again

Do not fear that driving, urging spirit
force which rises deep within your
being and yearns to set men free!
Now claim all of your children.
Bear the full weight of responsibility for
all of them—
red, yellow, black, or white!

Do not hide, but tell them of their history—
hiding nothing—
for in your face I see a blinding light of glory,
in your spirit I see a broad ray of hope.
And men shall have their hope restored and
the land shall have its glory restored as
your joy and laughter echo across your nation.

And the full life of my sons will rise
and outlive the death of my fathers' sons.
And the full, rich wombs of my daughters
will carry and bear and birth the children
and make seed rise from the embers
of your abortions and your celibate monasticism
and your pain.
And the vibrant strong seed of my sons
will implant themselves in willing wombs
and supply the seed that once their forefathers—
like Onan—spilt in the
reckless, aimless, goal-less ground of past dishonor.

71

ones

Tell Me Again

Now grateful for the seed implanted there—
aborting not one!—
for already too much potential lies in the
ash heaps and the graves of our families' pasts.
Out of the warm womb of my praise and worship
I shall bear my sons and daughters—
my womb lined with the blood of all my mothers'
mothers,
now not spilt in wasted motherhood—and
not stolen by the seed-devourer.
And I shall say,
"Eternal Father, this child is Yours!
And this one! And this one! And this one too!"

Now, with boundless faith in their destiny,
every seed of mine—and yours!—
will find their place in this land.
And to their God and my God they will declare,
"This land is my land.
This land is Your land, Lord."
And the glory of the Lord will be revealed!
"As He spake to our fathers,
to Abraham, and to his seed for ever."

around your **neck** and write them on your **heart**

Tell Me Again

Part 3

"I hear the sound

of children's voices..."

SAVE *the* CHILDREN *of the* WORLD

Sometimes I hear God say,

"I hear the sound of children's voices, laughing, crying, calling out My name...
They watch and wait...they crouch in fear...they linger in the shadows of your nations' streets...
Their voices come to Me from the damp, musty ghettos of Rio's dark and musty barrios.
They come to Me from Sarajevo's tattered tents.
They come screaming to Me from Detroit's noisy projects."

Yes! It is the same piercing cry, the same hollow laughter, the same plaintive call.
Everywhere there is the molester's beckoning finger, the seduction and the pain, then shame, guilt, and fear.

what is

the fast

I have

CHOSEN?

75

Tell Me Again

Alcohol abuse is evident in 35 to 70% of physical abuse cases.

Everywhere there is the treacherous older friend,
his threats, his beatings,
then the child's entrapment, his slavery, and
bondage.
Everywhere the night's fitful sleep is shattered by
the cold rain, the hungry rats,
the intrusive body part of an exploiting, ravenous
rapist...
and yes, first the screaming sirens, then the
attacking lights,
then the swift rush of biting, chastising, deadly
bullets.
And then comes the silence of the night as we
clutch our dead,
and listen for a lost heartbeat...

76

Everywhere the running, forsaking mothers, with tired, dry
breasts,
with heavy hearts, abandon us...

Everywhere are the angry,
crazy, shouting, cursing,
and frightened, helpless
fathers whose hands
bring slaps and shame,

Tell Me Again

whose feet bring kicks and who always stay away
so long...

shouldn't

"How well I remember...the day the police came
for my older brother, and the night they shot my
father and raped my mother."
"How well I remember the cold, dark, back
rooms—of the cold, dark foster homes of the
greedy, scowling, foster parents...."
From chaos, hunger, and shame they go to terror,
slavery, and fear!

you be

No voice but ours—yours and mine...
Never a voice have the children had—no voice but
ours; theirs are...

undoing

77

voices muffled and silenced by
cold instruments of death
voices muffled and silenced in
the crib by disease-infested,
dirty milk bottles
voices muffled and silenced by
stinking breaths and sweaty
hands
voices muffled and
silenced by stray

the

heavy

BURDENS?

Tell Me Again

*Approximately 25% of the deaths caused by child
maltreatment involved parental substance abuse.*

bullets of angry police
voices muffled and silenced by powerful, sleek
molesters
voices muffled and silenced by silver-tongued,
lying lawmen
voices muffled and silenced by inciting, provoca-
tive jailers
and then sooner or later by the cold, but alas, not
always cruel, hand of death.

No voice but ours—yours and mine...
No Father but ours—yours and mine...

And how *His Father heart* beats with the desire to
care and love and bless His children, to watch
them grow in wisdom, stature, and fullness!
How His Father eyes roam to and fro, watching
them as they stumble and fall, and rise and reel,
and fall again under the painful attacks of the evil
one who, with audacity and mocking laughter,
attempts to make God's children his own...

"And while the Church primps and pampers and
nourishes and enriches its adult self;
And while its hollow, empty, cheerless praises rise
pitifully to the echoing ceilings; and
while it speaks so glibly of His impending coming
to 'bring release,'

Tell Me Again

"My Father heart breaks...
It breaks for the empty
hands that come with-
out their children.
It breaks for the empty
Wombs that corrupt
themselves with death,
with such empty excuses.
It breaks for the empty
words that speak so hol-
lowly of self.
My Father heart breaks for
the aborted anointing that
wastes away in many a
father's spirit—
an anointing that should be passed down to a
waiting son,
an anointing that generates itself and produces
new life within a son,
an anointing waiting to become the lifeblood of
its new generation...that anointing lies buried in
some father's grave!"

79

then...

your light

will break

FORTH

and you will see

HIS GLORY

Tell Me Again

God will have

His quiver full!

A Prophet's
RESPONSE

Tell the nations how God will remove His glory from them, because of the broken covenants.
Declare to the people the curses of God upon nations
that reject the next generation
that murder their unborn children
that make little provision for their children's education
that turn a blind eye to the fathers' callousness
that turn a deaf ear to the children's cries
that continue to enslave their children in labor camps, in homes, in factories, in brothels, in sweat houses
that welcome sex tourists and foreign investors looking for cheap labor
and that destroy God's heritage and reward.

81

Prophesy of a better day
when the children's voices of laughter will be heard
when the brutish ones will be destroyed
when the cry of the women will cease
when the voice of the bridegroom and the bride
will be heard in our land
when virgin daughters will not be despised
when sons will no longer be eunuchs in Babylonian palaces
when seven women will not have to lay hold of one man
when no loss of children and no widowhood will
break the women's hearts
when more will be the children of the married
wife than the children of the desolate...
when even God will have His quiver full!

Tell Me Again

your children reap

what you have sown

Let it shine.

The GRIEF of GOD

If you quiet your spirit and listen carefully...
this is what the Lord says:

The blood of the children slain rises to My nostrils and their muffled cries come to My ears. You hear and you forget, your senses dulled by your own pain, your eyes reddened by your own crying, and refuse to turn in the direction of the grief—your grief, yes, and *Mine*!

Your children reap what you have sown. The next generation absorbs your pain and struggles with your loss, and writhes under your beating.

What then shall I do with you? How shall I turn your hearts to Me? How shall I reveal Myself to you? I have waited long for this nation to turn to Me. I have waited long for the moment when you could grow up as adult sons and daughters and inherit My vision for you and for your nation. I have heard the cries of your people and I have seen your shame, your reproach, and your loss...

And now I turn to you and now I bare My heart to you. For indeed I can no longer wait for you to turn your hearts to the children. So I shall avenge Myself of My own adversaries and the land will hear the cries, and see the blood, and fear their faces, and wish that it had never given birth or that the orphans had died imprisoned in the womb!

Then I must wait...for another generation of a nation's fathers to break the curse and set My children free, and then to present to Me, blameless, the trophies of My joy and My pride—My children.

83

Tell Me Again

Let it shine.

The Generations

Inseparably linked to one another by obedience to the will of the Father

GENERATIONS of seed, not ruled by "blind" obedience, rule instead by sighted obedience.
Wanting only to please the Father, they say, "Not my will, but Thine be done!"
Walking without a backward look at what could have been, they go ever onward to accomplish the will of the Father.

Child of promise, I would quickly teach you of your purpose. I would brush away your childish tears.
But still I would prod you on to obedience.
You would love God's law and deeply it would be imprinted in your spirit.
You would eat that Word until its bitterness would become sweet to your taste.
You would honor the path your fathers have taken,
and you would honor also the will of the God of your fathers,
and you too would become linked—by your obedience...

Obedience to the will of God—this is the missing thread, the link that connects my seed to the God of my fathers.
I will give that seed air to breathe of the sweetness of the Father's life
—to drink deeply of His will
—and to want nothing else but to do that will.
And with purpose and no backward look, my child will walk toward obedience—the death of his own will and the life of his Father's **WILL!**

Tell Me Again

85

Over 2.9 million child abuse reports were made in 1992.

why di rum shop—dem cram

tell
me
again...

an di church—dem empty

A Caribbean Child Contemplates Life

TELL ME AGAIN

tell me again
why tings gone so bad
and why some people jus hold dem head and bawl
and why even di preacher, dem only talking about
how bad tings get
and all di while some people money still pilin up
in di money-market
while some people t'iefing for a livin
an others jus lie down by di roadside
ready to die!
an no shoes on di pickney—dem foot
tell me again

tell me again
why di rum shop—dem cram
an di church—dem empty
an why di big people—dem fat
an di pickney—dem t'in
an why in God's earth the bad-talkin people—
dem don't jus shut up dey mout if dey don' have
nothin good to say...
tell me again

87

the Kingdom of God will be given to a generation producing

ITS FRUIT

Tell Me Again

*Approximately 53% of child victims
are female and 46% are male.*

tell me again
why everbody sayin it can't work
but nobody doin anythin about it

tell me again
why is di same ole story I hear from all di big, big
men sayin
how di country gone bad
an di politicians worse
an how even dog can't get cornmeal
an how I can't get schoolbooks an...
an Jesus, what You goin to do about it, eh?

once

you

were

An all dem lookin fat and eatin
  good,
    an wonderin how an where
    nex to save dey money—
    an still payin di poor people
    dem minimum wage
    tell me again!

not

tell me again
why some people so rich an
why some so poor
    an why some say "Lord, di
    groun' no level at all!"

a

PEOPLE

88

Tell Me Again

an why some people work hard and some jus
plain lazy
an why di chaff will burn and di wheat will not
tell me again

tell me again, Daddy,
why some people forgive and others do not
an what Jesus mean when He sey "seventy times
seven"
an I can't even count, much less multiply!
an why some people sey "I'm sorry" an some sey
"I don't care!"
an why God sey I mus forgive my friend an den
turn roun' an forgive my enemy too
tell me again

tell me again
why Jesus sey if a man t'ief yu coat give him yu
jacket too
an I don't have one coat an never own a jacket in
mi life!
an why Jesus didn't answer one word when His
enemies tell so much lie on Him
an why sometimes I feel someting like a hot fire
rushin up inside me sayin, "It's not my fault!"
but then how come I feel so warm inside whenever I give somebody someting or when I jus
listen, or when I jus turn and walk away...
tell me again

89

Tell Me Again

*More than three children die each
day as a result of maltreatment.*

tell me again
why little chickens follow Mother Hen
an why all that proud Cock can do is make a
whole heap a noise wen mornin come!
an why some parents forget that we children fol-
lowin dem
an why even wild animals feed their young
an why God sey He is goin to smite dis earth wit a
curse...
tell me again

tell me again
why people so diffrent
why some so short an some so tall
an why Adam was di father of all
an why some people "rob Peter jus to pay Paul"
an why is only one earth, one Father, an one way
that everbody laugh—from the inside out!
tell me again

tell me again
why deep down in my heart there's a song
why little birds like to sing an the clowns like to
laugh
an why people shout an hit each other an walk off
without waitin to hear "I'm sorry"

90

Tell Me Again

an why this ole
earth is groanin,
groanin like a
woman tra-
vailin to born a
baby
an how one day it
will laugh—like if the
pain was nothin at all!
tell me again

...in the

tell me again
why nobody listen to the wise old people
an why everytime we forget an keep doin the
same old thing
that hurt other people
an why the ones who listen and the ones who
remember
an the ones who stop hurtin other people
have so little to regret
an so much to enjoy
an so much to laugh about
tell me again

day

91

when

I make

up My

JEWELS...

Tell Me Again

*In 1991 most child abuse reports were
made for children under the age of one.*

Jesus took a child up in His

Suffer the little children to come unto Me

arms and blessed him

BLESSING
Like Jesus Did It

HERE is one way to restore God's image in a child: Jesus took a child up in His arms and blessed him. At one time the disciples attempted to "protect" Jesus from the thronging children. Jesus' words—so often quoted, but so little understood—was a clear rebuke as well as an unequivocal statement of His position concerning children. *"...Suffer the little children to come unto Me, and forbid them not: for of such is the kingdom of God. ...And He took them up in His arms, put His hands upon them, and blessed them"* (Mk. 10:14,16).

93

Tell Me Again

Among substantiated victims of child maltreatment, approximately 44% suffered neglect.

THE blessing of a child invokes the restoration of God's image in a child. Jesus' frequent blessing of children must have gone something like this:

"I bless you, My child, in the name of My Father, whose image you bear. I bless you that you may always keep that spirit of laughter, humility, and joy. I bless you with abilities to be a worthy citizen of God's Kingdom. I bless you with the bountiful blessings of God My Father. I bless you with the knowledge that you can come to Me whenever you wish. I bless you, My child, and stamp again My image upon your spirit, soul, and body."

94

Part 4

tell me

again

and God heard

the cry of the child

One FATHER, TWO Women and SURVIVAL

97

Two women, two sons, two nations, and a God who loves all His children... Sarah gives Hagar to husband Abraham so that he could father a promised son. Hagar obediently bears the "outside" son Ishmael. Things change; barren Sarah still remains childless. Jealous Sarah despises and pompous Hagar "has an attitude." Sarah at last conceives and births the promised Isaac. Hagar and son Ishmael still ridicule...

Tell Me Again

Among substantiated victims of child maltreatment, approximately 24% suffered physical abuse.

and Sarah still makes Abraham
agree...to send the "other" woman and
her child away.
Abraham gives them some food and
water and exiles them to the desert.
All the food is gone and a brokenhearted
mother leaves her son to die and weeps
before the Lord.
"And God heard the cry of the child."
And God quickly intervenes. "Get up!
Take up your son! See, over there is
water!"
And Hagar's sons still cry...
for water from their Father.
And Sarah's sons still laugh...
for water from their Father.
And the Father of Abraham's children

thy

wife

SHALL BE

SHALL BE

Tell Me Again

*still hears the crying and the laughter
and calls on weeping mothers—
wives or bond-women mothers,
married women or "other" women
mothers,
Sarah, Hagar, or Keturah mothers—
to pick up all of Abraham's dying
children
and go find that pool of water,
to laugh with all of Abraham's laughing
children,
and go claim all of Abraham's rich
inheritance!
For all of Abraham's children have a
blessing from God!*

99

VINE

VINE

Tell Me Again

*Every 13 seconds a child is
abused in the United States.*

a call to care...

let
them
hear
the
call...

...for a nation's children

the cry to the
NATIONS
and their leaders

I see it in the eyes of my nations' leaders:
a sense of loss, a sense of failure.
I hear it in the words of my nations' leaders:
a sense of loss, a sense of failure.
I hear it also in the songs of the Church's people:
a sense of failure, lost hope, lost paradise,
the will to survive only, but not to conquer
the will to dominate within, but not to dominate
without
a sense of escape to the courts within
and to leave the brokenness of the world without
a sense of preservation of that which is our own
a sense of preservation of our weak selves
and a shunning and a shirking of the greater
vision,
of the greater call
with no desire to dream—for dreams only
demand that we lengthen our days, that we labor
for the prosperity that visions always seem to
demand!

And I hear the weak and adult Church
struggling for answers, but not willing to embrace
a new vision
not willing to interpret their dreams, nor

Tell Me Again

101

*Among substantiated victims of child maltreatment,
approximately 2% suffered from medical neglect.*

yet the dreams of the nations' leaders, for those
very dreams demand that we are to preserve the
dying, famished nations.
Those dreams demand that we receive the blessing of the firstborn—
yes, that which brings us wealth, but also that
which brings with it the responsibility for the
rest—the dying world, the hungry children...

And when I look into the heart of God
I see a desire, no, a craving, for dominion. I see
the vast, great love of the Father,
I see His hands outstretched to love and care for
His people,
I see His hands outstretched to wrap His children
in His arms and be a Father to them
—not the reproach of scoffers who proclaim His
death, His inability to procure change, or His
unwillingness to change the plight of the world's
lost ones!

How their cries, the cries of the
little ones, rise up to Him!
Their brokenness, their pain, their empty hollow

cries, their dull hoarse laughter—
the children...
orphaned by the ones who bore them, and
orphaned by the world's injustice,
orphaned by the hardship of their parents.
They are orphaned by the hardheartedness of a
world that itself does not care if it lives or dies
and so does not care for the little ones
whose life would mean that it too would have to
keep on living!
And so it did not feed the little ones whose preservation meant the prolonging of its life of pain
and loss.
And then I hear again the weak call of the Church.
I see the weak aims of the Church as we so hope-
lessly speak of the little ones and so "water down"
the food with which we nurture them!

103

But today I hear God's call for you to dream
and for you to bring your strong little ones
and let them hear the call of God upon their lives;
a call to dominion;
and for you—
a call to fatherhood,
a call to care...for a nation's children.

is the
LORD

Tell Me Again

*In the United States, at least 4,000 children
die each year from physical abuse.*

a good man lays up

an di
children
still don't
have no
name...

children

an inheritance...

nothing FOR YOUR children

They have no name, no paternal links,
no history of who their fathers were!
No father's name is on the birth "cerfiticate."
One young boy only heard that some slave-master broke the back of a young, strong son of an African prince, coveting his woman...and stole that young boy's great-grandmother's private womanhood.
And another only knows that his grandfather's grave lies under the guango tree by the village church,
and "He was the pastor too!" some say in whispers.
And a young girl still tries to figure out where that strange European name came from and how come...?
And another young boy still has trouble explaining how come his hair is so straight and his nose so flat...

Tell Me Again

In 97% of reported cases of physical abuse, parents are the perpetrators.

Some fathers wait around long enough to take the second step—to wed the little woman to "take away the shame" and "give the boy-child a name"...

But wen di hard time come an wen di
pickney—dem a bawl out fi hunger
an wen di greedy landlord come knockin down di ole
front door
an di pot still tun down in di cupboard—
den dat young man sey im "soon come"—
sey im gawn a-look wuk
an Lawd know—sey im still don't come back yet!
An all di time all di man—dem still a sit down
under di plaza, playin cards
wid dem hungry belly
an di politicians crave di votes of di fathers an
mothers
an scheme fi the pow'r of the union workers
an "one han rub di other"
an "money pass unda di table"
but still di mothers get no help at all.

Tell Me Again

An still di school—dem
have no window an hardly
any door
an di children still don't
have no name
an no father to claim...
an still the hearts of the
fathers tun to the
"big people"
who wuk money an vote on election day.

107

And the children roam the streets and steal
our fruits and wash our windscreens
and drop newspapers in our yards and mow
our lawns
and eat our leftovers and scrub our pots
and sit in our "back rooms" or on our roadsides and wait...

For the hearts of their fathers to be turned
toward them.

But those children never forget all those old
stories their grandmothers told them—
all about sweet Africa, or those smelly
sailing ships.

Tell Me Again

60% to 70% of runaways, drug addicts, and prosti-
tutes report child sexual abuse in their backgrounds

Like that one about the fine, tall Frenchman who came a-courting Grandma, but who stayed only long enough to...nobody ever told them what went on in the front bedroom. Only one day the Monsieur was gone and Grandma's eyes were red...and I think he took the gold too...and he didn't leave her anything except three children: one black, one white, and one in-between. And the teacher could hardly pronounce their last names—and so the other children laughed and the nick-names stuck long, long after the galloping sounds of the Frenchman's horse were echo-ing across the sugarcane field.

108

And no father's heart was turned toward his children.

Or the story the little mamma told them...
Dem sey the ole man had good money
dat im used to wuk on di massa banana
estate and
den dem give im job as di foreman an
den him wuk di likkle piece—a lan dem gi im
an how im tun over di money an buy more lan and
den...INHERITANCE

Tell Me Again

den one day di priest come in im long white robe an
smellin like incense
an sey dey well need some lan for di new church
an how dey will mek a pew wid we name pon it, special, special
way inna di front of di church for we to sit on.
An so di grandmother sey wid her mouth tight,
tight,
jus like di knots she tie up di handkerchief wid di
money,
"Dis lan is for di church!"
An now—not one inch of lan lef fi di children
an I still sayin to myself dat God could-a neva
want dat lan more dan di children need it!

109

Tell Me Again

exploitation...

...and a nation's cry

They are weak,

O Africa!

O Africa, sweet motherland,
heaving with the groans of all your children,
your heart pulsating with hope for one lost
generation after another,
your breasts sore from the hungry mouths of
your hungry children,
you tied your waist and straightened your
back and braced yourself to carry the weight
of all the pain and loss.

111

And the massa still slaps your fathers down
and the land still yields the best to those who
own it
while those who work that soil get only the
scraps that fall off the table...

And the ones you thought would come from your
own loins
and the sons you scraped and scrimped
for, to send to that foreign school

Tell Me Again

but He is strong.

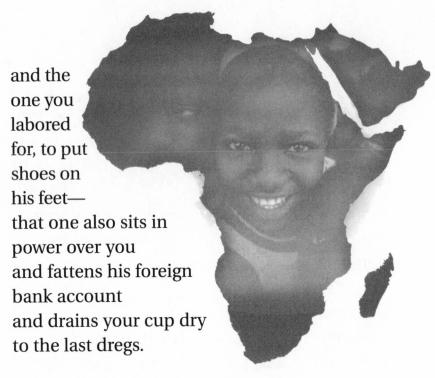

and the
one you
labored
for, to put
shoes on
his feet—
that one also sits in
power over you
and fattens his foreign
bank account
and drains your cup dry
to the last dregs.

112

And still you wait…you wait for your God alone who
would lift the burden and take some of the load
and help you put that burden on the shoulder of
another…another generation…

And your children still laugh…they play
childish games
around your skirt…
They mock their hungry bellies.
They defy the wasted breasts and the empty baskets.
And their laughter still rings out.
It is a sound of hope!

Tell Me Again

And your men...they make that land quake
under their determined footfalls,
they squeeze out a living from the broken
cisterns,
and still square their shoulders
and still lift their eyes and look for the cursed
fig tree to yield its fruit.

And when the nighttime comes,
they join together their voices
and talk under the guango tree...of the good
old days,
and good women and sick children and the
"t'iefing, advantageous massa" and the hope
for rain...tomorrow!

113

And this one good woman wonders if she can
bear
the weight of all the nations' pain.
And she too defies her empty breasts.
And she too strengthens herself
to bawl out, loud and long, the wailing of her
women
to shout out, loud and clear, the voice of

Tell Me Again

her people
to write out, bold and plain, the pain and the
loss and the cry of the people...
and to crisscross your nations and kick down
those hellish gates...

"Here, widow woman—take back your child
alive!"
"Here, exploiting massa!—Take this! And this!
And this!"
And I shall still have strength for my own dear
children
the children of my nation, sweet Jamaica
and of her sisters, Trinidad and Tobago.
And I shall awaken my people and
turn the hearts of the fathers back to the
children.

I wait and I long for a better day of sweet
tomorrows
when miracle child after miracle child will be
preserved alive
and descend with life from that once receptive
womb.

114

I wait and I long for a better day of sweet tomorrows
when the sound of the bride will match the sound of the bridegroom
and with eager longing, they will make their babies and watch them grow.

I long for a better day when
the childish laughter of childish children
enjoying their bestowed childhood will be heard on our playgrounds and in the open marketplaces.
And that innocent laughter will come from roadsides once feared
and from ghettos once hated
and from bedrooms once prisons...
transforming laughter, glorious and childlike!

115

Tell Me Again

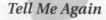

Physical abuse is the single greatest cause of death in infants between 6 and 12 months.

a
nation
a nation
nation
whose
fathers
sold it to
the evil one...

A Nation's Cry Against the OCCULT

They ravish the women and the children of my nation. They turn upon themselves, driven by the evil one. They defame themselves and inflict upon themselves the pain of lost generations. They shame their sisters and ravish their mothers, strike down their fathers and thrash around in their own death grip, and welcome death, which brings relief.

A nation gripped by the teeth of death, clawed by the burning fangs of suicide, devours itself and devours its seed.

It is a nation whose fathers sold it to the evil one, whose women wallowed in its muddy pools and offered up their children as sacrifices to the fertility gods, hungry for the blood of all their children, blinding their eyes and entrapping them in dark ignorance, illiterate and barefooted...

And still from the deep belly of your land, I hear the groaning and the travailing in pain until your sons, no longer sold to satan, no longer forced to collect the wood for sacrifices, stand at the top of every street and manifest their sonship, shouting,

"This land is my land! This land is Your land, Creator *God!*"

Tell Me Again

At some time during their lives, about one in two females have been victims of unwanted sex acts.

God see everythin

an hear everythin

A Caribbean Child Contemplates Life

TELL ME AGAIN

tell me again, Daddy,
tell me again, why that rich powerful king with
that big farm got such a cravin for Naboth's small
farm,
an why he ask that poor farmer to sell him the
only small piece of land he got...

tell me again
why even when Naboth explain how he had to
keep the land to pass it on to his children, that
that greedy king jus take the land anyway...
an why the jealous king got more jealousy and
why Naboth had no jealousy at all...
tell me again

119

tell me again
why the rich king got richer and why the poor
man got poorer
an why the powerful king got more power an why
Naboth had no power at all...tell me again

tell me again
how that God see everythin an hear everythin
an how one of these good days Naboth and his
children will look down from the bosom of
Abraham
an how that ole greedy, Dives king will beg them
for just one drop from Naboth's children's
well on Naboth's children big, big farm!
tell me again!

Tell Me Again

*About 80% of child sex offenders fall
within normal intelligence ranges.*

A Prayer for the
NATIONS' CHILDREN

Pray this prayer daily:

"Restore Your image, Father God,
in these our children, and Yours.
Rise from Your throne and set Your broken children free.
Blow Your Spirit-breath and bring new life
to the dying children.
O God of all the nations,
visit our nations with consolation for our children.
Touch the hearts of our leaders.
Turn the hearts of our fathers
back to the children.
Visit us with deep conviction, Lord,
and turn us toward the fruit of our womb,
and let Your Kingdom come
and Your will be done
as we carefully handle these tender rods of Jesse.
And we present alive again,
those fatherless sons to their widow-mothers,
and present to You, O Father Eternal,
all the children of all our nations,
blameless and favored,
Your children indeed,
stamped in Your image and
reflecting Your likeness.
In the name of Jesus, Amen."

121

Tell Me Again

*Long-term effects of child abuse include fear, anxi-
ety, depression, anger, hostility, and poor self-esteem.*

today God's call

tell me again...

is loud and clear

Restoration of Sons of Destiny

TELL ME AGAIN

the earth

This old earth, cursed with Adam's rebellion, groans and travails and reels in pain, waiting for manifested sons to rise and set it free!
Yet the very sons whose purpose is to set this captive earth free themselves remain captive to the curses of generation after generation of fathers.

groans

But today God's call is loud and clear and resolute! He will execute His divine intention. He has one way only—to crush once and for all the works of the dominion-craving evil one—and that is by raising up dominion-bearing sons, image-bearing sons, who walk in the glorious liberty of firstfruit sonship, who will call forth life to the groaning, travailing earth.

123

in

So tell me again...

travailing

PRAYER

Tell Me Again

65% of births to never-married women were from unintended pregnancies

Tell me again how come there is only one way you
know that this old earth will turn over in its grave
and resurrect with new life....
and that is when manifested sons walk freely
upon this land
and bring manifested glory of God's manifested
presence
to transform all of this death into brand-new life.
And manifested sons will speak life upon this
death
and manifested sons who know the battle songs
of that Lion of Judah will roar with dominion
authority and rally all of God's creation to heave
with relief,
and surge with new birth
and tremble with spirit life
and shake itself free at last from the long curse
of thorns and thistles and barrenness and blood.
And manifested sons will free their brothers and
their little sisters
and, uninhibited by fear or memory of lost
conquests,
unhindered by the threat of the scornful
adversary,
those sons will set free those broken, hurting little
brothers
and, free at last, all of God's children will sing the
glorious freedom songs of manifested sons.

WARRIOR

Tell Me Again

Tell me again how all that suffering, and all that
abuse, and all that crying
will be swallowed up in the victory songs of firstfruit sons
and the rich harvest of manifested sons
and the mourning will turn into dancing
tell me again.

Tell me again how they say that God Himself put
a promise rainbow in the sky,
and if it's true the angels sang "Joy to the world,
the Lord is come!"
and how God was really laughing out loud
when that old Pharaoh thought he could bribe
those Hebrew midwives to kill off all those sons
like Moses
and how God was really laughing
when that old Herod thought he could bribe those
wisemen three to tell that murderer where baby
Jesus was.
Tell me again because I love to hear how
David never died at the hands of Saul and
how captive Daniel prospered at the hands of his
enemy
and Joseph survived pit and jail and slavery
and how so many children survive so much abuse
and tell me how God will have the last long laugh
with all of His children flocking around His feet!
Tell me again!

Tell Me Again

125

YOUTH

*5.5 million children regularly do
not get enough to eat*

Tell me again how I've got a shoe and you've got a shoe and
how all God's children got a shoe
But why in Jesus' name some children not wearin
de shoes!
Tell me again.

Tell me again why I want to sing a new song that
long before I get to Heaven I'm goin to put on my shoe
and walk all over dis here earth down here
because de ground is cold and hard and
because when I get to Heaven I really want to
walk through streets of gold with my bare feet and
the truth is—
I really need those shoes down here!
Tell me again!

Tell me again how come the heel of the women is bruised
and the head of the serpent is crushed
and how come that means that we don't have to
fuss about a little bruisin now and then
—especially when dat satan's head has no life, no
teeth, and no power!

Tell me again how just like a little bruise on your
heel makes the whole body writhe in pain
just so the sufferin and cries of our brothers and

Tell Me Again

126

sisters make the whole body holler out its grief
and feel that things would never change...
Tell me again.

they shall

**Tell me again how we can't let a little bruise on
our heel keep us back from dancin with praise
or weaken our stompin on the enemy's head.
So tell me again that**
            is heal Jesus heal those bruised heels
            and is crush Jesus crush that satan's head
and all of God's children will one day dance like if
heels make to take a little bruisin
and the pain is nothin at all compared with the
feelin that I feel when that old serpent's head is
under my feet!
Tell me again!

127

but they shall

*Psalm 8:2 says the sound of the children's praises
will still the enemy and the avenger. As the praises
of a restored group of children are heard in our
streets, as with the sound of the Pied Piper, many
lame, bruised, and abused children will join with
them in songs of deliverance. It will be a liberat-
ing experience for the weakened Church and for
God's world of children in trouble.
Tell me again.*

enemies in the

Tell me again how come you had a dream
dat everywhere you look was dark, dark, dark,

GATES   *Tell Me Again*

*400,000 youngsters carried a
handgun to school in 1987*

and everbody hidin in dem houses and "batten
down" dem windows
and all de big people dem lock up demself fright-
en, frighten
and nobody walkin in de dark, dark street.

Tell me again how come from far away de happy,
happy sound of children singin come floatin
down
like sunshine in de middle of de day...
tell me again.

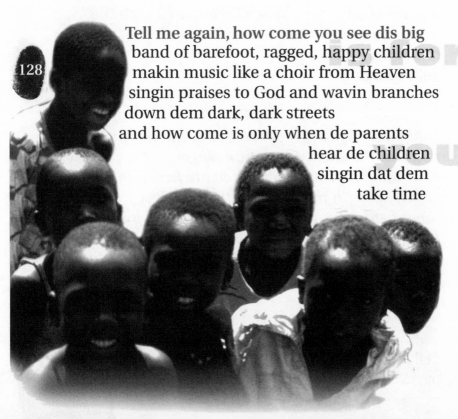

Tell me again, how come you see dis big
band of barefoot, ragged, happy children
makin music like a choir from Heaven
singin praises to God and wavin branches
down dem dark, dark streets
and how come is only when de parents
                    hear de children
                    singin dat dem
                    take time

128

Tell Me Again

crack de window dem and peek through de crevice
and de more dem hear de children praisin is de more brave dem get to turn on dem light and open dem windows.
And **tell me again** how is only dem hungry orphan pickney dem singin dat make darkness turn to light and dismal gloominess turn to joyful freedom...

tell me again
Tell me how is dose same little sufferin children dem
dat God will use to change dark, dark houses and dark, dark people and
glory! glory!
Tell me again if is true dat old satan he has to flee and
how God Himself get up and sing and dance with the little hungry praisin children dem

129

...tell me dat one again!

ANOTHER

Tell Me Again

Every four hours a child commits suicide.

"Out of the mouth of babes and sucklings hast Thou ordained strength because of Thine enemies, that Thou mightest still the enemey and the avenger."
Psalm 8:2

Sources for Statistics

Advance Data from Vital and Health Statistics of the National Center for Health Statistics, No. 189 (Sept. 26, 1990)

American Psychiatric Association

Global Child Health News and Review, 1995 (State of the World's Children)

Global Child Net, 1995

Kids Count Date Book, 1994 (Center for the Study of Social Policy)

Lewis, et. al., 1983, quoted by "The Invisible Victim: Children of the War at Home," Family Prevention Fund, 1991

Morbidity and Mortality Weekly Report, Vol. 43, No. 50 (Dec. 23, 1994) Centers for Disease Control and Prevention

National statistics from ChildHelp USA
    NCPCA, 1993
    Violence update, 1993
    United States Department of Health and
       Human Services, 1993
    CCPCA, 1992
    David Finkelhor, 1986

United States Department of Justice, 1991
Diana Russell, 1986
Briere, 1992
Herman & Hirschman, 1981
Browne & Finkelhor, 1986
Patterson, 1992
Mendel, 1993
Voices, 1993
Burgess & Groth, 1984

1995 figures from Children's Defense Fund

Protecting Children in Cyberspace, a Vancouver
Police Union Charitable Foundation
Check, p. 17
Brodkin, p. 44
Ruddy & Fairholm, p. 8
Wolfe, quoted by Fairholm, p. 108
Schmitt, quoted by Fairholm, p. 108
Badgely Report, quoted by Ruddy & Fairholm, p. 8
R. Summit, quoted by Ruddy & Fairholm, p. 8
Finkelhor, 1986, quoted by Fairholm, p. 149
Finkelhor, 1986, quoted by Fairholm, p. 167

Runaway statistics from Operation Go Home

Technical Analysis Paper, No. 42, U.S. Department of
Health and Human Services, Office of Income
Security Policy (Oct., 1991). Authors: Meyer and
Garansky

Index

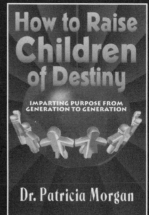